MW01016901

69 DAYS IN THE NICU

my lovely Lina
love you so much
God·bless you.

69 DAYS IN THE NICU

Akeir M.J

© 2017 Akeir M.J
All rights reserved.

ISBN: 1546718591
ISBN 13: 9781546718598

ACKNOWLEDGEMENTS

*M*y deepest appreciation and thanks go out to the following:

- *The Alberta NICU doctors and nurses. You have been the greatest! Thank you for researching the best medical plans for our babies. We were at peace knowing that our children were well taken care of when it came to being medically treated.*

- *The Neonatal Transition Team, for coming to our house, carrying heavy bags full of equipment to take measurements and weights for our baby.*

- *The nurses, who took their time to explain all of the medical terms, which were completely foreign to us. I am forever grateful to you. Thank you as well, for the many shoulders that I, Akeir, deposited tears on.*

- *The social workers who stood with us in this difficult time. I will never forget your kindness, and your passion to help a grieving and frustrated mother. Your hard work was very much appreciated.*

- *My loving husband, Joseph, who was my rock and support throughout. I love you with all of my heart. Thank you for understanding me and not giving up on me.*

Thank you for being the father each child wishes for and thank you for being the husband every women longs for.

- *My beautiful children, Joshua, Blessing, Ruth, George, and of course, Joy, who really started all of this. Thank you for your patience, as I was away many days living at the hospital.*
- *My editor, Michelle Baily, for making me look like a professional writer. Thank you for your sacrificial time of hours spent on this manuscript.*

-Thank you to my Apostle Elhadj Diallo and his lovely wife Nadia Diallo for being the amazing spiritual support to me and my family.

- *Everyone who has invested in this book by reading, purchasing, or drawing from my experience, to better go through theirs. May you be encouraged into that place where you will fully understand the journey that you are on, and make the decision to never give up on your dreams.*

Though it may be difficult for some to read through this, it is my hope that my story will bring inner healing to you, as it did to me while writing this account. I can now open up a new chapter of my life.

So, fasten your seatbelt, make a cup of tea, snuggle your baby close to you, relax, and be comforted by the words of these pages.

-Akeir Jal

TABLE OF CONTENTS

ENJOY READING!

PREFACE

On October 19, 2016, I was encouraged by a young woman whom I had met at the South Health Campus Hospital (Calgary Alberta), to write about my journey of having both a premature sick baby and a premature healthy baby. A week later, a dear friend of mine for over ten years, asked me if I had ever considered writing a book. I knew then that I would have to share my story with other mothers who have gone through, or are going through the pain of living in a cold hospital, and facing the loneliness as I did. There are the struggles of hearing the negative medical news almost daily regarding their child's condition, which then follows with that confusion of why their baby is even sick. This then brings on the fear of death, and the reality that their infant may not pull through.

No one understands the pain of labour, or the unthinkable pain of losing a child more than a mother. It is a bitter pain that no words can express. No pills can take away that kind of sorrow, and no money can bring back a deceased child. There are no perfect funerals which can offer a grieving mother the peace of mind that she so desperately wants. There are no words to wash away the memories of her horrifying journey.

I am not writing this to discourage anyone, but on the contrary, to encourage, and to bring awareness to the pain and struggles that mothers will inevitably go through, when they are faced with this reality. I am writing to share my story, and to commend and commiserate with all mothers who have had a premature baby, mothers who have lost a baby because of prematurity or sickness, and mothers who have lost hope, because the family now has to live in the hospital with their newborn. They now are sadly faced with that possibility that their child may have to remain in the hospital's care, and that they may never go home.

I am writing to share my painful moments of leaving these facilities, with only the choice of trusting the doctors and the nurses to take care of my baby.

In this book, I will share my desires as a young woman and my journey to reach my dreams, my happy ending, or as you may call it, my destiny. I will share my jubilant, sad, bitter, and disappointing experiences along the way to that destiny. I will be candid, and share all of the pain that I struggled through, as well as the heart breaks that no mother should ever have to endure. I will focus as well, on the tears of joy that were gained, even though this suffering and confusion was so hard to endure.

One moment, everything was fine, but then, in a matter of seconds, everything had crumbled to dust. The dreams and desires which I had, suddenly vanished, and all the hope which I had gained, disappeared, and my laughter turned from joy into sadness and mourning.

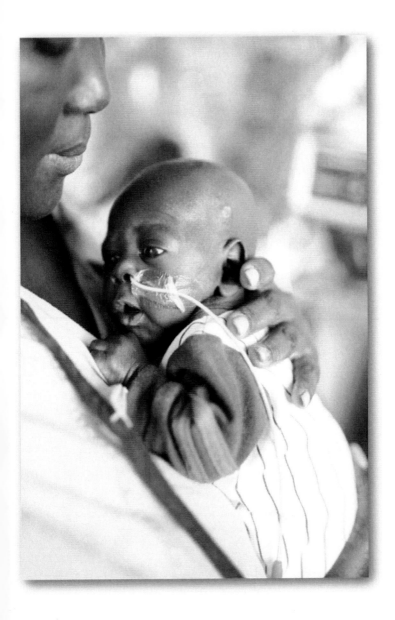

CHAPTER 1

A YOUNG GIRL'S DREAM

Even from the young age of fifteen, I knew that I wanted to have four children: two boys and two girls. I remember telling my friends and family members that one day, it would happen.

I had come from a large family of 13 children, so I thought it would be best to narrow down my expectations to four children for my sanity's sake.

In 2002, I met a handsome young man, who simply asked me out, and I said, "Yes." The rest is history, and on August 12, 2006, we were married. Two years later, we found out that we were pregnant with our first baby.

It was my belief that pregnancy would be easy, and it is for some, but like many other women, this was not the case for me. It was a difficult time for the first few weeks, because of always being sick, even to that point of feeling like I was going to die. My body was out of control, and with pregnancy, it affected even the simple things, such as the texture of lotion on my skin, which was not the normal feeling that I had pre-pregnancy state. As well, I would have to sit as much as possible, because of the dizziness, where the world seemed to be continually spinning around me.

Following that three month period, which seemed like an eternity, all I then wanted to do was eat, sleep, and just be lazy.

After about three months of this, I felt trapped, and started to wonder when these nine months were really going to end. I went from a routine of being very active to a routine of laziness, where I would rest with every chance that I had available to me. The tiredness was overwhelming, that even at work, I just wanted to sleep.

I should have asked questions to give myself a heads-up, but that was not the case. I thought, "What could ever go wrong? I don't need other people's opinions. I can do this." I was trying to be super woman, and suck it up, so to speak.

It was with that mindset that I didn't ask about labour or the things that I would need for my baby. Sometimes, it is best to just ask those who have gone before you. My mother used to say, "If you would have asked, would it have killed you?" I used to argue and say, "Yes. It depends on what you ask, because it might just kill me." She would shake her head and walk away, knowing that one day, I would come back to her and say, "You were right, mom. It would not have killed me if I had asked."

The worse transition was when I went from a small size to an extra-large. I can remember a time where my husband took me shopping, and I instinctively went to a medium section, erroneously believing that I still had my pre-pregnancy shape. I was soon faced with my disappointing reality. I found out that I was no longer small or medium, but extra-large in size. I went to the change room and burst out crying, making everyone in the store wonder, "What is wrong with her?" I was so sad that I could no longer fit into anything but extra-large clothing.

In addition to this, I experienced a sudden and dramatic increase in estrogen and progesterone, as well as changes in the amount and function of a number of other hormones. These changes did not only affect my moods, but they also created that glow of pregnancy, and significantly aided in the development of the fetus. These hormones altered the physical impact of exercise and physical activity on my body. At first, when my doctor was explaining this to me, I felt like he was speaking a different language, but since that time, I have come to fully understand.

It is a sacrifice to be a mom, and I finally realized how much my own mother sacrificed herself for nine months to give birth to me, and with this realization, there came a new level of appreciation for her. From the day I gave birth, I started honoring my mother, loving her more, and understanding her even better.

CHAPTER 2

LABOUR AND DELIVERY

On the morning of August 30, 2008, I was scheduled to be induced into labour at 7:00 AM, as I was already overdue by four days. That morning, I woke up with all the energy in the world. We were told prior to the birth that we were having a boy, and I was so happy to finally meet my son. I even put on make-up, because I wanted this baby to exclaim and think, "Wow, my mother is beautiful."

We arrived at Peter Lougheed Centre (NE Calgary, Alberta), where there were many women being admitted for delivery. I used to think that women just walked, screamed, and then pushed their babies out. At least, that's how they sounded and looked to me. I turned to my husband and said, "I think I can do this. Just go in, scream, and before you know it, we will have our son." He looked at me and said, "Okay baby."

Soon after admission, I was taken to the triage area, where one of the nurses came in and gave me a list of the different kinds of painkillers that were available. She then asked me which medication I would prefer when the labour pain really began to kick in. I can remember her questioning me, "Would you like an epidural or laughing gas when your contractions require intervention, and if a natural birth, would you like a hot bath?" Without thinking, or asking further questions, I said, "No thank you. My mother had her first baby in a village all by herself at the age of sixteen, and so, if my mother could do it, I think I can do it too." The nurse said, "Are you sure ma'am?" I said "Yes." She reiterated by saying, "In case you end up needing any of the medications, please let us know."

Never compare yourself with anyone, not even your mother. The strength she has or had, may or may not be the strength you have.

A few minutes later, the doctor came in, and before we proceeded with the induction plan, he said, "Let's break your water and see how things go from there. You might not need an induction after all, if you go into labour naturally, which would be perfectly fine." He then proceeded to break my water, and moments later, I felt a pain that I had never experienced in my life. Now I understood why painkillers were provided! The agony was so severe that I did not want to stand, sit, walk, or lie down.

I felt like urinating in between crying, screaming, yelling, and praying. I was in so much pain that I was confused. At one point in the process of labour, I screamed my mother's name asking her to forgive me for not listening to her when I was younger. I repented of all my sins, and prayed to God in hope that this pain would disappear. I forgave all my enemies in this dramatic state.

I didn't want my husband to say a word or even breathe out loud, because I felt that if he said anything, the pain would only increase. After all, this was his fault! At that point, all I could think of was that nurse with the list of painkillers. I screamed, "Where is the medication? Bring me the epidural now!"

Suddenly, the Anesthesiologist came in to inject me with pain medication. I was so happy to see that man! That was the day that I fell in love with epidurals. The agony was finally gone and my husband could speak to me again!

Labour was complicated due to the fact that the baby was sitting higher than normal, and that he also was sound asleep inside, because I had eaten a large pizza sandwich just before labour. The nurse tried shaking my stomach, and asked me to move around, in hopes of waking him up. We tried all that we could to rouse him from his sleep, but it was to no avail.

I would strongly advise any woman not to eat anything before being induced. This may cause your baby to have a heavy nap and slow down the process of labour. Drink fluids, and eat yogurt, fruits and/or crackers if you are very hungry, but stay away from heavy foods.

After 48 hours in labour, I ended up having a Caesarean Section, and on August 31, 2008, at 12:45 PM, our perfect son Joshua, was born. My bad experience in the labour room almost changed my mind about having more kids, until I saw my baby's face. He was a healthy eight-pound bundle of joy, and he was beautiful!

His handsome little face gave me strength and hope, in that I would live through another birthing process in the future, because that reward in the end is indescribable. I fell in love with him, and I forgot all about the pain and drama that had just transpired.

After I had freshened up, I started apologizing to the nurses and doctors who had to put up with all of my antics. You would think that a woman would just give up because of a bad experience, or a life and death situation in the labour room, but no, we go ahead and we do it again! Why? It is because there is a passion inside of a woman, which drives us to do it again, a passion that is really never satisfied. A woman with this kind of desire does not give up, and she doesn't back down, or surrender to her problems or struggles that come along the way. Women always have a plan B in place. A woman can give up her whole world to pursue her desires, and to reach her destiny.

Two days later, we were released to go home, and honestly, I had no clue of how to take care of a baby. One of the nurses tried helping me with instructions of what to do on my own, but realistically, mother instinct would have to kick in.

Within a week after leaving the hospital, I had contracted an infection, and had to be readmitted to the hospital for monitoring. The hardest part for me was when baby Joshua couldn't stay with me at the hospital due to the shortage of beds. Imagine the feeling of excitement in just giving birth, to that of total despondency.

CHAPTER 3

WHAT'S WRONG WITH MY BABY?

Two years later, we became pregnant again. This time, I was more confident. I knew what I was getting myself into, and moreover, I knew what to expect. I was so happy, and I couldn't wait to see this baby. We went for the regular 12-week ultrasound, where we were taken to a quiet dark room. As we entered this area, my heart began to beat very fast, but I was unsure as to why.

The radiologist started taking measurements, which seemed to be taking longer than usual. Forty-five minutes had passed, and she was still in the process of measuring things.

It was then that I asked, "Is everything okay?" She said, "Yes, the baby is just not in a good position." I was not buying what she was saying, and I immediately sensed that something was wrong. Always listen to your instincts. When something is not right, you will definitely feel it, and most of these times, you will be correct.

The radiologist then excused herself and came back with a doctor. They both proceeded to take measurements for another fifteen minutes, talking amongst themselves as they did so. Finally, the doctor looked at both my husband and myself and said, "Something is wrong with your baby." He went on to say that they needed to run more tests, and that it would be best if we could go to the Radiology Department at the Foothills Medical Centre. (NW Calgary) Of course, I wanted him to explain in more detail exactly what he meant by 'wrong,' but he said that only after the additional tests were taken, could they verify what was seen on the ultrasound.

I was not completely concerned at this point, because nothing was confirmed as yet, but I was very restless. I kept on thinking and over thinking of what could be wrong.

A week later, we were back for another ultrasound. This time, the doctor performed the procedure himself, and confirmed that my baby had club feet, and that the ribs looked like they were very weak, to the point of breaking. In addition to this, the baby's airway also looked very narrow. The first question that ran across my mind was, "Why?" Question after question then followed. "Why me? What did I do? How could this be?" Our lives completely changed after these results.

Tears began to roll down my face, as the doctor finished explaining our baby's prognosis. I didn't know what to do, or what to think. I didn't understand how to accept such painful and discouraging results. The doctor then took us to another room and waited for us to calm down. He went on to say that he would strongly recommend us to terminate the pregnancy as soon as possible. If we didn't choose this option, we were told that we might not be able to have more children in the future, due to the damage that a broken bone could cause inside my uterus.

At this point, I had mixed emotions and I wasn't thinking straight. I had an interesting stare, or so I've been told. My mind said blink, but I couldn't blink. My dear husband was trying to be positive with encouragement, by telling me that everything would be okay, and that he was here for me, and that we would get through this together. It was sweet of him, as some have said, but I was so confused, upset, and shocked, that I didn't want anyone to talk to me, or to touch me. I knew it was not anyone's fault, but I needed a moment to search my heart, and to calm my nerves. We went from driving to the hospital happy and talking, to a complete, silenced drive home.

C H A P T E R   4

TERMINATE MY BABY?

This was a hard pill to swallow. I kept on asking myself if I had heard the doctor correctly. I turned and asked my husband, "Did the doctor just say, terminate the baby?" My husband replied, "Yes."

In the ancient world, abortion was freely practiced, and so, abortion is not a modern phenomenon. Surviving texts from the ancient Greco-Roman world reveal that ancient people were well acquainted with abortion. It was discussed by doctors, philosophers, lawyers, historians, and poets. Some found the practice to be good and necessary, while others found the practice to be evil and contrary to nature.

Those who promoted abortion had a variety of reasons: to prevent unwanted children, to reduce the number of weaker children, to hide sexual activity, to prevent bodily disfigurement, to reduce the number of heirs, and to avoid the expenses and burdens of child-rearing.

Today, women over forty are encouraged to abort their pregnancies due to higher risks of infants being born with multiple complications. Many women in this age category choose to carry their babies to term and do have perfectly healthy children.

I would like to encourage every woman to reconsider the option of abortion, due to your baby being sick. Search your heart, and give yourself a few days to think and pray about it, because it is a human life that you are about to end. Some women have unhealthy relationship issues, such as abuse, which is totally understandable as you make your decision, but I urge you to seek counselling before making this permanent choice. As there are so many women who are unable to have children, adoption is a viable option, if you are unable to keep the baby after carrying to full term.

Abortion for me was not an option however, and so I requested another ultrasound for a second opinion. This time, I saw everything that the doctor had described. The doctor suggested a test called an amniocentesis, which is a medical procedure used in prenatal diagnosis of chromosomal abnormalities and fetal infections. It also determines sexual gender before the usual eighteen week ultrasound. A small amount of amniotic fluid is drawn out of the abdomen through a needle, and this fluid contains fetal tissues, sampled from the amniotic sac surrounding the developing fetus. The fetal DNA can then be examined for genetic abnormalities, such as Downs Syndrome.

After being informed of this procedure, I immediately felt very uncomfortable, which led me to refuse the test. The doctor then gave us two weeks to think about the option of terminating the pregnancy.

After hearing the heartbeat of the baby, there was no way whatsoever that I could even think about ending my baby's life. My husband and I called the doctor's office and said that we were not going to terminate the pregnancy.

The doctors tried all that they could in helping us to understand the dangers and risks of carrying the baby to possible full term. They said that if we were to keep the baby, my womb could be severely damaged by the broken bones. He continued by saying, that giving birth at full term would mean a Caesarean Section.

After that, we would only have a few short moments to see and kiss our baby, before the struggle for breath would begin, and our baby inevitably would die. We were told that the baby's narrow airways would take two to three minutes before closing completely, so we would need to make sure that we said our goodbyes quickly. Imagine saying goodbye after being pregnant for so many long painful, discouraging, disappointing and emotional wrecking months, and then, only having two to three minutes to say goodbye.

I lost sleep, as I was always crying, and so sad beyond words. My son felt this change as well. Our home went from one of happiness and laughter to one of constant mourning, for a baby that had, at that time, not yet been born. My husband was so supportive, because he knew what this meant to me. I just couldn't stop the heartbeat. If it was going to stop, then it had to stop by itself, in its own time. I believe babies are a gift from God according to Psalm 127:3.

After 18-weeks, we went to find out the sex of the baby. As my husband was driving to the Foothills Radiology Department, my heart was beating again, and this time, I was afraid that I would be forced to terminate the pregnancy, if they were to find more things severely wrong with the baby. I couldn't bear to hear any more bad news.

When we arrived at the hospital, more measurements were taken, and we were told that we were having a baby girl. This made me even sadder and more frustrated. A boy and a girl is the million-dollar family. Many couples wish to have these kinds of odds.

In my sadness, the questions remained center in my mind. "Why would this happen to me? Who did I offend to deserve this, because I was willing to ask for forgiveness? Have I done something wrong for this to happen?" Unfortunately, though, there were no clear answers. I prayed and prayed, in hopes that something would change the next time that I went back to see the doctor. I wanted to scream, yell and run, but I had to stay calm, because I didn't want to have a miscarriage. I felt hopeless and helpless, and very confused with these painful results. As well, our son started to notice that mommy was always sad, and he would come and wipe away my tears, which were always unending.

CHAPTER 5

BROKEN WATER

At 35 weeks, my water broke. "What? Why? How?" It was as if what I was going through was not enough. Stress and restlessness was written all over my face. I was confined to bedrest at the hospital for two weeks. While in bed trying to save this pregnancy, my mind and my heart was not at peace. All I could see or hear was death. All I could think of was that I had two to three minutes with our baby girl, and then we would have to say good-bye to her. I didn't want to say goodbye. I didn't want her to suffer at all. I just wanted to hold her and to never let her go. I wanted to give my world for her. Goodbye was not an option, therefore I wanted time to stop just for a moment, and I wanted favour from God.

I am sure that there were some people who thought that if I didn't want her to suffer, then why wouldn't I just end the life inside of me, before she would have to feel any pain.

Everyone has their different way of thinking and handling personal or family matters. My choice was to see her, love her, and let her know that she had a family that cared for her. We would not let go of her just because of this sickness or possible death.

It is still painful, even as I write this with tears rolling down my face. It seems like it was just yesterday, for the memory is still so vivid.

What would you do if you found out that your dreams were being crushed into pieces? Would you give up, or would you keep on trying, and fight for your dreams to come to pass? I fought and fought to see my child recover, despite the negative prognosis.

Two weeks later, I was released to go home, but was still confined to bedrest. I was happy at first, because at least, I could be around Joshua and he wouldn't have to come visit me at the hospital. After coming home it was even harder than I thought it would be, as I was not allowed to do anything, but lay down and go to the washroom. This definitely was not my nature, as I am very active. There was a time where I felt like I was robbing Joshua of his happiness, as he would have no choice but to play with his toys and watch TV until his dad got home from work.

After a couple of days of being at home, I realized that my hospital bag was not ready, so with the help of my dear husband, we were able to pack essentials that were needed. I initially started packing when I was a little over three months pregnant, but now I wasn't sure if I should take the bag with me, as I would only have minutes with our baby. Every time that I touched this bag, I would stop and cry because I knew that possibly, that bag and the blanket that was inside, would be the only things that would come home with me if the baby passed away.

Four days later, I went into labour. The pain this time was just as unbearable. I remembered the words of my mother saying that there was no ultrasound back in her day, all the way over in Africa. The only way to know if the baby was a girl or a boy, was from the different areas where the pain started. If you were having a girl, the labour would start from your lower back and abdominal region, and the pain would be very rapid. That was exactly how I felt, and if you're having a boy, contractions are strong, but slow.

I was in labour, afraid and confused, and I felt very cold. I kept asking for warm blankets, while thinking of what I would say to my daughter, and how I would even hold her, because she would be so delicate. I kept on praying in my heart that a miracle would happen, and somehow, she could live a little longer, so that her brother could meet her.

Early in the morning of June 17, 2010, around 5:30 AM, baby Joy was born naturally. I thank God that I didn't have to go through another C-section. She was 6 pounds, and beautiful with curly black hair and big round eyes. She was fair, and looked exactly like my mother, her grandmother, which made my heart glad, because of the great relationship I had with my mom.

Joy entered this world crying, but the strange thing was that we couldn't hear her voice. I was waiting and waiting to hear her cry. I panicked and started weeping.

The room had at least four NICU (Neonatal Intensive Care Unit) medics in attendance, and three doctors. Surprisingly, the doctors' plans had to change, because now they were dealing with a baby that appeared to be healthy.

Only two things were noticeably evident. One was that she had no voice, and two, her feet were clubbed.

I ended up not getting my two to three minutes of time with her, as she was taken away immediately, with her dad right by her side. I had no idea what was going on. Everyone was so busy, and no one was saying anything, which I took to mean that 'no news is good news.' I was hopeful now that there was a better chance of Joy living a little longer than what had previously been the prognosis.

CHAPTER 6

A SURPRISING MIRACLE

Yes! It was a miracle. At this point, I was so happy that Joy didn't pass away in those first few minutes after being born. I took a moment to thank God for answering my prayer. I couldn't wait to get out of the labour room. I wanted to tell the nurse that we could do the post labour routine later? I just wanted to go see my baby.

The doctor came back a half hour later, and said that they had to intubate baby Joy, but that she was doing amazingly well.

I asked the doctor what 'intubate' meant. He said that it is an emergency procedure that's often performed on people who are unconscious or who can't breathe on their own. A flexible plastic tube is placed into the trachea, or windpipe, through a person's mouth or nose to help with breathing.

He then went on to tell us that the genetic team was coming later in the day to run more tests. I wasn't really interested in who was coming or going. I just wanted to get out of the labour room and see this child that I had been waiting for. I wanted to hold her, and keep on holding her.

After the doctor stepped out of the room, I wanted to fly. I felt like the wheel chair was too slow for me. I was telling my husband, "Why can't you just push the wheelchair a little faster?" I was forgetting the fact that I had just given birth to a six-pound baby girl.

Joy was resting in an incubator in the NICU room at the Foothills Hospital. The moment that I saw her, I could not hold it in, and I began to cry. I was not allowed to hold her, due to all of the intricate wires hooked up to her IV line. She also had a feeding tube, intubating machine, and many other contraptions that were foreign to me. I was just glad that she was alive, and that was all that mattered.

Hours later, our son was brought in to meet his little sister. He looked at Joy, and smiled. I burst into tears, crying so hard, because I wanted Joy to come home one day, and play with her big brother. Seeing her with all of the wires connected to her little body, I knew that it was not realistic for the doctors to allow her to come home anytime soon. This created a hopelessness in me, which left me emotionally weak. Every time I thought of Joy, tears just flowed down like rain.

I was released three days later, and I was also introduced to the NICU world. It is one thing to give birth and take your baby home, and another thing to have your baby taken into the NICU with serious complications.

The last thing that I wanted to do was to leave my baby at the hospital with people that I didn't know. There were more questions like, "Who are they? Do they have a baby? Will they be careful with her? Will they remember to feed her? Will she be comforted when she cries?" I didn't want to trust anyone. I was afraid that she might be neglected because her voice was mute when she cried. All kinds of anxious feelings were running through me, but I didn't need to worry, because the nurses and the monitors were doing a great job.

The hardest time for me was in the middle of the night when I would wake up, and my baby was not by my side. In order to check on my child, I had to call the hospital and talk to a nurse, who usually did not know me. I am still grateful that she was there though. After talking to a nurse, I would feel so good in knowing that Joy was sleeping, and that everything was still fine. Unfortunately, though, it would only take a couple of hours, before the concern would set back in, and I would have to call the hospital again. Restlessness seemed to engulf me on a regular basis.

After those hard nights at home, the next day would arrive, and I would be back at the hospital visiting Joy, walking down the cold, lonely, halls.

I saw many mothers during this time, walking with their heads down, and this would make me sad. Some would be crying and others were taking their babies home. It seemed like it was regular life for the hospital and for the people, or maybe they had just adjusted to this.

Fear is a normal reaction to the unknown. Most parents have little previous experience with sick newborns, and many are uncomfortable in the NICU environment. They may also fear the possibility of serious illness, disability, or even death. They can begin to question their own abilities to take care of this ill or premature baby. It's okay to fear, especially if it's your first baby or the first time to experience a NICU environment.

Some parents also fear their friends' and relatives' response to the birth, and mothers in particular, can sometimes worry that their partner will blame them for a complicated birth, which could lead to the loss of the relationship.

Having a sick child or premature baby is not your fault. Stumbling blocks can turn into stepping stones. If I had not gone through this, I would not be writing this book. I would have no way of explaining the feelings that I have just described. I saw the other parents taking their babies home. I saw mine remaining in the hospital.

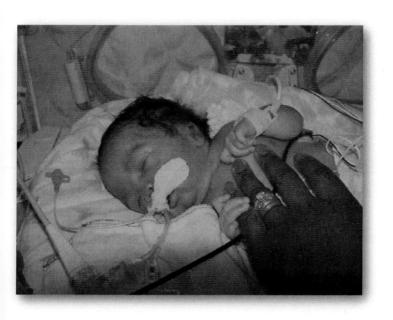

CHAPTER 7

DIAGNOSIS

When I saw Joy, after the first separation, she seemed to be okay. The nurses were taking good care of her, which gave me more assurance in the fact that they knew how to do their jobs. All the negative thoughts were starting to finally settle. Shortly after I arrived, the genetic team came to assess Joy for a few minutes, which was something I became accustomed to over time.

A week later, Joy was diagnosed with Osteogenesis Imperfecta type two.

Osteogenesis Imperfecta Type Two? What in the world is this disease? Why and how did it even connect with me or my husband? I had no idea of what it was, and had never heard of this abnormality.

It is most severe, and frequently lethal at or shortly after birth, often due to respiratory problems, numerous fractures, and severe bone deformity. Small stature with underdeveloped lungs, tinted sclera, and improperly formed collagen are typical characteristics of this disease. People with this condition have bones that break easily, often from mild trauma, or with no apparent cause.

According to history, this condition, or types of it, have had various other names over the years in different nations of the world. Among some of the most common alternatives are Ekman-Lobstein Syndrome, Vrolik Syndrome, and the colloquial Glass-bone Disease. The name 'osteogenesis imperfecta' dates back to at least 1895 and has been the usual medical term in the 20th century to the present.

We were questioned as to if there was such a condition in either of our families, where we both responded, "No." Unlike my lack of questions regarding labour, I took time to ask why she would have this condition if this came through her genetic make-up. We were told that it was not necessarily a hereditary genetic disorder, because genes could sometimes be altered by a mutation, causing a change in the structure of the genes' DNA. When a mutation occurs, it can disrupt the normal functioning of a gene. This is what happened to my daughter Joy.

This explains why, at twelve weeks, her ribs appeared weak and that they were possibly breaking. The doctor was explaining to me that infants with this condition have breathing problems, and have a short life expectancy. Children with this disease are expected to die at a very early age. Thank God that she lived after birth.

I didn't know what to think or to say. Fear of Joy passing away, due to this condition, scared me. A social worker was called in to help me through this painful realization, but I refused to talk to anyone, nor did I want to see anyone. I just wanted to be alone, which looking back, I realize was a very bad decision.

Holding on to your fear and anxiety, which causes emotional weakness, can catch up to you, and ruin you along the way. I became so sensitive that anything would make me cry. Funny jokes only brought more tears. Try to express your thoughts and talk to a friend, husband, or a nurse, if you are not comfortable with the social workers.

CHAPTER 8

TRANSFERRED

The doctor said that we needed to be transferred to the Children's Hospital the next day. The reason for this was that Joy needed to have a Laryngoscopy done. I, of course, asked what that was.

It is a flexible viewing tube that goes through the nose and down to the throat, to check for any issues in that area. Joy did get the Laryngoscopy done, and the results were not positive. Her throat was swollen, which narrowed her airway, and was exactly like the initial ultrasound had depicted.

Joy needed urgent treatment for her swollen throat due to being intubated. The fastest medicine that would be effective in just a few hours is a drug called Dexamethasone, which is a type of steroid medication. This helps in reducing the swelling of the throat more rapidly. After three days of this treatment, she had another Laryngoscopy done, and this time, the results were more positive, even though her throat was still narrow.

From June 2010 to October of that year, I was battling with myself, in trying to accept the fact that she would soon be gone, but a part of me strongly believed and had faith that another miracle would happen, and that all this heartache would go away. I had sleepless nights, mostly because she was away from me. A mother who wants children cannot, or will not stay apart from her child.

My pillow was soaked with tears every night. If tears were counted or stored, I think I could have filled a bathtub, or the house itself.

Sometimes I would wait for my husband and son to fall asleep, and then I would slowly go into the bathroom, lock the door and just quietly cry, because I didn't want them or anyone else to comfort me. I just wanted to cry. My heart was so heavy and my mind was so tired. I needed to just cry to relieve me heart from being so heavy of sadness and restlessness.

CHAPTER 9

EXTUBATION

On October 20, 2010, we were told that if Joy survived being extubated, we could be released and take her home with an oxygen tank. Before she was extubated, the doctors told me to hold Joy in case things did not go as expected when they removed the tube. The tube was the only thing that was separating the two sides of her throat and when it would be removed, there was a 99% chance that her airway would collapse and that she would have difficulty breathing. If this happened, then there would be nothing that anyone could do at that point. The doctor would give medication to Joy to help her relax without struggling, and so that she could die peacefully.

Can you image hearing such words? Many of you have heard this, but it is in the believing of these words that will alter the outcome and the process in which you walk it out.

I said, "No, can you take the tube out on her bed?" My husband and I had such strong faith that she would live after they took out the tube. The doctors looked at us with dismay, because they believed that there was no chance of such a miracle. Well, miracles do come true, and believe it or not, she lived, and came home, just as we had prayed that she would.

I was so happy when we were released to go home, and our son Joshua was overwhelmed with joy. He wanted to hold his sister at all times. Most of the nights while she was at home, I couldn't sleep because I felt that if I slept, something might go wrong and she would pass away. I was constantly living in that fear of death.

CHAPTER 10

DEATH

On November 3, 2010, around noon, after cleaning and cooking, it was Joy's lunch time. When I tried feeding her, she refused to eat, so I began to sing to her, because she liked music, and would sleep every time she heard it. As I was singing, she breathed, then paused, and then took another breath. I contacted my husband, who was in school, and he immediately left to come home.

In the meantime, I called the ambulance, and listened to the instructions from the lady on the other end in how to give CPR. My body was shaking as the tears flowed from my eyes. I felt like her life was literally in my hands at that point. I was giving her CPR, knowing that I could lose her at any minute. The ambulance finally arrived, and they took over from there, not even allowing me in the back with her, which was more than I could bear.

We were rushed to the Children's Hospital. As soon as we arrived there, the doctors were waiting for us. They tried everything that they could, but to no avail. She was struggling to breathe, as she kept looking at me, as if to say, "Goodbye mommy. Don't cry. It is time for me to go."

A few minutes later, our beloved Joy passed away. She died so peacefully, and looked as if she were only sleeping, and would wake up anytime soon. The room felt so cold and there was dead silence.

Shortly after, my husband and Pastor Elhadj Diallo, who is now an Apostle, arrived at the hospital. Apostle Elhadj had and has been with us through thick and thin, and has been there every step of the way through this entire ordeal, never saying that he was ever tired or unavailable.

I couldn't believe it was over. I didn't want to let her go. I mean, how could I let her go? Lying on the bed, how could I just walk away? I was screaming, saying, "At least take me to where she is going, because she might wake up and no one will be there to hold her. I am willing to be right there by her side when she wakes up." Joy was, and still is my baby and she will forever be remembered.

There were no painkillers to help me relax when I lost my child. I will never forget her eyes. She had such beautiful eyes, and was just perfect to me. Remembering her peaceful state on the hospital death bed, would often help me through, and it still does.

Leaving the hospital after Joy's passing was the hardest, leaving it difficult to walk. When we entered the vehicle, our son said, "Where is baby?" Again, I just burst out crying. In fact, if it wasn't for my husband, I would have ran back to the room where I had last seen her, knowing that the next time of our meeting would be at her funeral, all alone in a box, and going somewhere dark. Mommy would not be there to hold her, or to kiss her and tell her that it's going to be okay.

I remember saying that I wanted to die in her place. Losing Joy was not supposed to be part of my mother-hood journey. Losing her, naturally made me think twice of having more children. I just wanted nothing to do with being pregnant or talking about a baby.

I had restless nights, where I would want to call the hospital and check in on her, but then, a few minutes later, I would remember that she is no longer with us. Every three hours, I would wake up thinking that it's time to feed Joy, but then would realize that she is gone, and that there was nothing that I could do about it.

A few days later, we had Joy's funeral. She looked beautiful, but cold, and my heart was torn apart see-ing her in the casket. I really wanted to hold her, pick her up, and never let her go. When it was time to bury Joy, I couldn't bear to see my little girl being put in the ground. I simply turned away, because I didn't want to live, knowing that Joy's body was in a hole. I wanted to remember her just resting in peace. In spite of how I felt, a part of me is so grateful that she lived long enough to come home. I am grateful that our prayer was answered.

After Joy's funeral, it was then that my husband be-came completely torn apart. He kept to himself, and was very quiet, showing frustration at times. Men mourn differently than women. There were times that he would just go for a drive in order to feel some relief.

A few months later, Joshua asked me the question, "Mommy, where is Joy?" As he was looking out the widow, I called him to come closer to me, where I then told him that his sister had passed away. He responded with, "Did she go to heaven?" I said, "Yes." The question was never asked again.

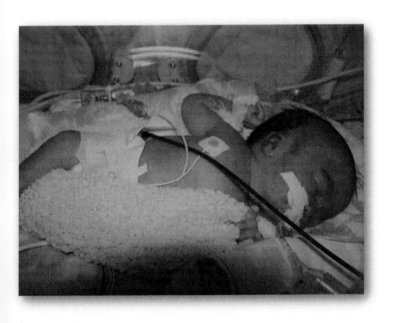

AKEIR M.J

CHAPTER 11

WHY ME, WHAT DID I DO?

Bad things do happen to good people, and you don't have to offend someone for bad things to come your way. Each person is born to fulfill a certain task on earth and no one said it was going to be easy, however, there are ways of coping with it, and that way will be up to you.

It is okay to feel normal grief reactions such as:

Feeling like you are "going crazy"
Difficulty Concentrating
Sadness and/or Depression
Irritability or Anger
Frustration and feeling of being misunderstood
Experiencing Anxiety, Nervousness, or Fearfulness
Feeling like you want to "escape"
Experiencing Guilt or Remorse
Ambivalence
Numbness
Lack of Energy and Motivation

Burying a child was not part of my dream. In all honesty, I have not let go of Joy, and writing about her reminds me of the pain all over again. Embrace all of your feelings and emotions. You're entitled to whatever feelings that arise, whether that be intense anger, guilt, denial, sorrow, or fear, all of which are normal for a bereaved parent. Nothing is off the table, and nothing is wrong. If the urge to cry wells up within you, just do it. Give yourself permission to feel.

Keeping your emotions locked up somewhere in your heart is just too hard. If you keep your emotions inside, you'll only make yourself feel worse about the saddest things you have experienced. It's perfectly natural and even healthier to let yourself feel everything you can about your loss, because this will put you on the path to accepting it. You won't ever fully be able to get over it, but you'll be able to build the strength to deal with the death of your child. If you don't embrace your feelings, you won't be able to move forward.

You could be a person who copes with the help of alcohol, or like my husband, who needed to drive around the city, with basically no destination.

Here are more ways to cope with your grief:

- Talk to family or friends
- Seek counseling
- Read poetry or books
- Engage in social activities
- Exercise
- Eat healthy, natural foods
- Seek spiritual support

- Take time to relax
- Join a support group
- Listen to music
- Be patient with yourself
- Let yourself feel grief

I kept myself busy, but not forgetful about what had happened. I trained myself to be thankful for the days that Joy had lived, and now, I can always remember our happy memories, which keeps me positive.

The only way that I am at peace with myself, is by believing that Joy is with God. I imagine her running around and playing in a place where there is no pain or medication. It is a place where there is no oxygen attached to her at all times. A part of me wants her back, so that she can grow and play with our son, just like I had dreamed, and the other part of me wants to keep her in that better place, where I believe that she is. The most precious thing of this whole ordeal is that we were all able to meet her and love her. She will always be a part of our family and our family memories.

Out of anger and frustration, I told my husband, who has been so strong for me and our son, that I didn't want any more children. He looked at me and said, "Your dream will be fulfilled. Just breathe. I am here for you."

I remember people asking me how I was doing, but it seemed like no one was asking much about my husband, so one day I asked him how he felt. He said that he was sad, and frustrated, but he understood why most of the attention and concern was towards his wife.

I am trusting that my story will strengthen another mother who is going through the same grief, the same pain, or a similar experience, such the one that I went through. I believe that this book will help that person know that she is not alone in her grief and sadness, and in remembering her loved ones. You are not losing your mind, and you will heal, but it is a slow process.

Father God, I am so sad and helpless I need you to strengthen me, I feel weak and powerless. In spite of how I feel I want to thank you for giving us Joy for this short amount of time, thank you because it was worth it. I give Joy back to you for I know she is safe and sound in your arms. can you tell her that her father and I did all that we could and that she is loved and will always be remembered. IN JESUS NAME AMEN

This was my prayer after Joy's burial.

Journal

_____
_____
_____
_____
_____
_____
_____
_____
_____
_____
_____
_____
_____
_____
_____
_____
_____
_____
_____
_____
_____
_____
_____
_____
_____
_____
_____
_____

Journal

_____

_____

_____

_____

_____

_____

_____

_____

_____

_____

_____

_____

_____

_____

_____

_____

_____

_____

_____

_____

_____

_____

_____

_____

_____

_____

_____

_____

Journal

_____
_____
_____
_____
_____
_____
_____
_____
_____
_____
_____
_____
_____
_____
_____
_____
_____
_____
_____
_____
_____
_____
_____
_____
_____
_____
_____
_____
_____

Journal

_____

_____

_____

_____

_____

_____

_____

_____

_____

_____

_____

_____

_____

_____

_____

_____

_____

_____

_____

_____

_____

_____

_____

_____

AKEIR M.J

Journal

_____
_____
_____
_____
_____
_____
_____
_____
_____
_____
_____
_____
_____
_____
_____
_____
_____
_____
_____
_____
_____
_____
_____
_____

CHAPTER 12

MORE BABIES

On January 3, 2012, I gave birth to a baby girl, whom we named Blessing, because that is exactly who she is to us. I was overwhelmed with happiness, and held her close to me every moment that I had. That was a habit that I had to break later, as she became accustomed to being held at all times, and would not sleep on her own.

I probably was a little paranoid, not wanting to leave her with a babysitter, afraid that something may go wrong, even though she was a healthy baby. I was very attached to her, soaking in all the moments of her growth. Blessing has such a loving and tender personality, but on the other hand, she can be very wild. She fills our home with laughter, and our family would not be complete without her.

On April 12, 2014, we welcomed another baby girl into our lives. We named her Ruth, and like Blessing, she was a full term pregnancy, with no complications in labour. Ruth is the funny one, who is extremely silly at times. She loves to sing, and is very serious about it.

On one occasion, she was loudly belting out her favorite song in a store, and we had to remind her that we were out in public. She began to cry, as there was no reason for this rude interruption on her heavenly performance. Needless to say, we do not interrupt her anymore when she is performing. Our two girls are so hilarious together, and their big brother adores them, even though they can drive him crazy at times.

This is not to ever say that I do not miss Joy. People may think that after a few counselling sessions, and having family around, that things would eventually go back to normal. Counselling and family support is very vital, but things don't ever go back to normal.

There is always that fear of losing another child or a loved one. The thoughts and experiences will never be erased from the mind of a mother. Even though I am blessed with three beautiful children, my heart is still broken. Sometimes I can't help but cry, wishing Joy was around, and that I could see her for a few minutes, for then my heart would be satisfied.

Shortly after Joy passed away, it was in this time period that I decided to continue my education. I had always wanted to become a social worker or a counsellor, and so, I earned my Bachelor's Degree in counselling on April 22, 2016.

Despite the sleepless nights and background noise of my kids playing while I wrote my essays, another part of my desire in life was accomplished. I was busy with moving on, and life started to be sweet again. To my surprise, it was at this time that I discovered that I was pregnant again, 6 weeks along, with my fourth child.

My husband and I were happy when we found out that another baby was on the way. We wanted a boy, and so did our son, and so, we prayed that this would be a baby boy.

CHAPTER 13

ANOTHER PROGNOSIS

I went for the normal twelve-week ultrasound and, to my shock, the Radiologist was again taking longer than usual to do the measurements, which could only remind me of the experience with Joy. The doctor came in after and said, "There is a light on your baby's heart, and I need to run more tests to make sure that it's not something serious." I said, "This can't be! More pain and suffering? Why?"

How would you feel going through a similar experience twice, but with different results?

This part of the book will touch on many medical terminologies, terms of which I had no knowledge of and had to ask questions about. It is here that I will share another painful experience, but this time, it is one that ends with good results. By the strength that I received through my pain, with the constant reminder of my late baby Joy, I will share how I coped with the struggle of another journey of confusion and frustration.

After hearing the doctors results, I felt like I was the only mother experiencing this pain and heartbreak, and would continue to ask, "Why me? Who goes through pain and battles to try to save a baby that might pass away anyway?" All kinds of thoughts were rushing through my mind. I almost forgot about the pain of dealing with another diagnosis and living each day with the thought of losing a child. The road of pain and suffering seemed to be endless for me. I was right back on that path to being emotionally wrecked and sad.

I imagined myself walking down the hospital's cold hallways again, with the doctors surrounding my baby. I imagined the genetic team coming in to make their assessments and final diagnosis. Flashbacks of monitor sounds, and nurses walking in and out of the room flooded my mind.

I still couldn't stop the flashbacks that came with every second, and it kept rushing through my mind.

"Would you go through this again? Are you going to make life easy this time and try to end it? Maybe I should just skip the doctor and ultrasound appointments? It might be best, so that I won't hear any more bad news."

A few weeks later though, I had to go back to the Foothills Radiology Department for an ultrasound to confirm the findings regarding the heart condition. The hardest part for me was waiting for my name to be called in to see the doctor. It was just nerve wracking sitting there with so many thoughts bombarding my mind.

The same doctors who encouraged me to terminate Joy were the ones that were there, and they remembered me. They felt sorry for us for a minute, but this time they were willing to support us on any decisions we were to make, even if the results turned out to be negative. They were willing to support my family in any way that they could. Knowing that made my heart glad.

The ultrasound revealed great news. The light on the heart that was originally seen, was disappearing, and their explanation for this was that the bright spot on the baby's heart was calcium that had developed in an inflamed area of the body, and that it would go away on its own. We also found out that we were having a baby boy. I went home very happy that day.

Our oldest son was overwhelmed with joy, because he was finally getting his brother. That day was the happiest day of my life. Hearing good news about a situation which was potentially negative, was a big blessing to me and my family.

WHY AGAIN?

26 weeks into my pregnancy, there was another turning point in my journey. It was an afternoon, where I was feeling very fatigued, tired, and emotional. A shower always helps me when I am in that state. The hormones were kicking in, and I was on the brink of tears, feeling extremely emotional and alone, even though I wanted to be alone. Pregnancy displays many facets of mood swings, and sometimes, you really don't know what you want.

After my shower, I went to lie down, but I felt as if my bladder were still full. This didn't make any sense, since it had only been five minutes since I stepped out of the bathroom. I didn't think much of this, as I headed once again to the washroom. It was then that I felt my water break. At first, I reasoned that I had urinated on myself, but when the full realization hit, I knew that this was not good.

I screamed, and my husband came to my rescue. He rushed me to South Health Campus Hospital, (SE Calgary) where I was then taken by an ambulance to the Foothills Hospital, due to the early onset of labour. It is in this hospital where they have the technology and tools to help babies that are born at such an early stage. Of course, they wanted to stop labour, and so I was confined to bedrest once again. Four days later, I was released to go home, but a nurse was assigned to come every week to make sure that the baby was fine, and that there were no developing infections.

I would like to thank whoever came up with the brilliant idea of having mobile nurses. God bless them so much.

It was an adjustment for my family in having a nurse come to our home. As the kids would see the nurse monitoring me, they would become worried that something was wrong with their mother, because they had never seen me ever lying down on the couch for more than a couple of hours. On the other side of it, staying at the hospital made me nervous, knowing that my children were at home without me.

This was very difficult for my mind to accept, and I would find myself always wondering what they were doing. "Are they okay? Has someone fed them? Did they take their showers? Did they sleep well the night before? How was school today and what did they wear?" It was question after question racing through my head, which would disallow me to sleep properly. I was so happy to be at home with them during this time.

CHAPTER 15

EARLY BABY #2

At 28 weeks and three days, on September 13, 2016, at 3:20 PM, baby George was born. He was a handsome, premature baby boy, weighing in at a whopping 1180 grams, which is two pounds and six ounces. Again, the doctors filled the room, because, of course, at 28 weeks, he was way too early to make his debut into this world.

The medical team rushed him away from me so quickly, so that all his vitals could be checked. I was immediately reminded of when Joy was rushed away as well. When I went to see him in the NICU, I will always remember his bed number as 23, right next to where Joy's bed was, (number 24) at the Foothill's Hospital in Calgary. I freaked out, and began to cry, which seemed like nonstop. My painful journey of **69 days had just begun.**

George was in an incubator, and he had a machine called a CPAP which had a mask to help him breath. This contraption provides constant air pressure into the lungs. George was on 21% room air.

The CPAP helps babies' lungs to develop without the baby having to work hard to breath, eat, and grow all at the same time. It is this machine that just makes life easier for premature babies. Again, I had to leave another baby at the hospital, just as I had to leave Joy not very long ago.

One instance when I was going home after leaving George at the hospital, I remember walking down the hallway of the NICU, where I suddenly became dizzy and fainted. I recall that there was a young man walking with his wife, who came to my rescue. It was a strange feeling waking up in the emergency department recovery room. To that young man, who I never met, and to all the nurses and doctors that came to my rescue that day, thank you so much.

I began to go through the same scenarios of having my baby in the hospital during the night, while I was at home trying to sleep. Imagine that feeling? Every couple of hours, I would wake up and cry bitterly, which would then follow with a call to the hospital to check in on George.

Three weeks later, the doctors were amazed by his growth and oxygen levels, and so, they decided to transfer him to South Health Campus along with the CPAP contraption. Once he arrived there, the CPAP was to be removed. This excited me, because, up to that point, his little face had been covered with tape, feeding tubes, and CPAP wires. I was finally going to see his full face.

When we were admitted to South Health Campus, George was admitted to bed number 29. The forward plan for him was to learn how to bottle-feed, and to grow to a healthier weight.

Within a week, George's breathing seemed to be different, and without wasting time, I immediately got the nurse's attention. Not long after this, the respiratory team took charge. Something was wrong, as you could hear his breathing becoming worse every minute. A half an hour later, everything went downhill, as his breathing pattern worsened. They repositioned him on his stomach, on his back, and on his sides, but nothing seemed to help. I could only watch anxiously, and believe that the breathing situation would take a hundred and eighty degree turn back to normal.

An X-ray was then taken, which showed that there was fluid in his lungs. The doctors discerned that this was the reason for his irregular breathing pattern. All that needed to be done was to flush out the fluid, and his breathing would or should get better. This was done, but did not change the direction of George's breathing pattern, which was escalating.

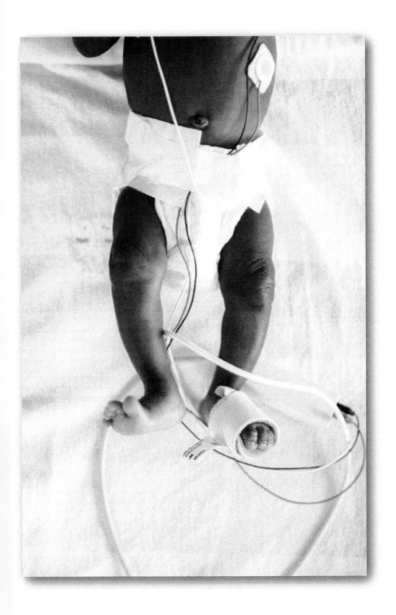

CHAPTER 16

INTUBATION REPEAT

Finally, the doctor said, "We can't take any more chances, so we will have to try higher pressure on the CPAP, and give him the 100% oxygen level, which is the maximum. If that doesn't work, intubate him."

I nearly fainted. I had to sit down, because I was having memories of Joy being supported by this very machine. I said to the doctor, "This can't be happening, not now. Please do something else."

Once again, my dreams were being crushed. The doctors had no choice but to intubate George and transfer him back to the Foothill's NICU. This time, he was admitted to bed 26. When we got there, I felt like we were starting all over again, back to square one.

Of course, all the nurses recognized George. I was continually telling myself that we were almost going home, but now there seemed to be no hope. I was frustrated again, and I walked with my head down, because I didn't want anyone to see me crying.

I stayed as long as I could watching all of the nurses' moves. I was restless, and again asking question after question. I thought that the nurses were getting annoyed with me, but I needed the answers. I felt like the wounds in my heart were being reopened, and it was even more painful.

One might think it would be easier the second time around, but it was more difficult. Reliving the fear and anxiety was horrifying. I was always on the edge, creating tension with my husband, who was always walking on eggshells, because I was so sensitive and unhappy. Anything that was said or done, would erupt the volcano and get me upset.

The next day, the doctor came in and said that it seemed like George was better, and it was best to put him back to room air, which means that he had to be extubated, and put back on the CPAP ventilator. The longer he was intubated, the more damage the tube could create, so they extubated him.

A couple of hours later, George was finding it hard to breathe as before. Here we go again. He had to be intubated, while many tests were taken to find out if he was infected by various bacterial growths. Antibiotics were started through an IV that was connected to the vein in his head. Baby George was getting worse day by day, although all the blood results were coming back negative, as there were no traces of any bacteria or viruses.

I was trying to think of what could have went wrong at the South Health Campus. In my anger and frustration, I wanted to blame someone for what was happening to baby George.

CHAPTER 17

MOTHERS ENCOURAGED

I would advise any mother who is going through a similar experience or trauma of any kind, to remember that the nurses, doctors, and genetic team are there to help with your baby's condition. You need their solutions, and they want to help.

While I was busy being upset and mad, they were busy trying to save my baby. Relax, and try to think clearly. Go for a walk, drink tea, call a friend, pray, and just stay positive and strong for your baby.

The doctor finally came to a decision that the best way to find out what was going on was by looking at George's airway, and determining if perhaps his airway opening was narrow and similar to his sister. This was possibly overlooked at the time of his birth.

Comparing Joy and George frightened me, because I could only think of Joy's ending, and I did not want George's conclusion to be the same. It was natural and normal to have these thoughts.

George's best option was to be transferred to the Children's Hospital. "No way," I said to the doctor. "I am not going back to that hospital. My daughter passed away there. You must do something here, please!"

At this point, my heart was beating fast, because in almost five years, I had not been to the Children's Hospital. I was afraid that the same thing would happen again and that I would, once more, be devastated, heartbroken, and disappointed.

I again asked myself if there was anyone that I had offended. "Had I done something wrong, and is God punishing me? Why is this happening to me for the second time? Was there a lesson that I missed from the past, and is it coming back to haunt me?" I was definitely the 'Question' queen.

My tears were pouring like rain, and I felt like there were so many of them, that I must have been created with an oversupply, because they flowed nonstop.

CHAPTER 18

FAILED INTUBATION

Things happened very fast after that. Once the doctors made their plan, the implementation took place within hours.

George was transferred, and admitted to bed number 29 at the Children's Hospital.

The doctors explained that when the respiratory team tried to intubate George the second time, they failed to insert the tube after numerous attempts. After five failed intubations, this could have been the reason for the swelling in his airway, which would account for his breathing difficulty. He went on to add that the best medicine that would quickly help to reduce the pain and swelling would be…but before the doctor could even pronounce the medication's name, I blurted out, "You mean Dexamethasone?" He said, "Yes," and asked me if I was a medical student. I replied, "No, but I had a baby girl who needed Dexamethasone."

He went on to say that in two days, they would have to perform a laryngoscopy on George, to indicate if there were any issues inside his throat.

Do you see where I am going with this? It was almost the same footsteps of Joy's journey. A few hours later, the medication worked so well that George extubated himself, by pulling out the tube at 3:20 AM. He stopped breathing for about a minute, and in this time, the respiratory team were trying their best to help George breathe.

I remember the head nurse watching the heartbeat and the level of George's breathing. She was urging the team to do something fast. Everyone dropped everything, and rushed to George's rescue, for which I will always appreciate. I was completely frozen. I couldn't think or talk at that point, as I was going through the shock and fear of losing another child. Deep inside of me, however, I had peace at the same time. I was so emotionally weakened, that my knees felt limp, and my stomach dropped inside of me.

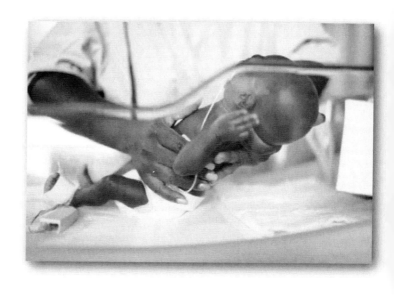

CHAPTER 19

BLOOD TRANSFUSION

George was thankfully put back on CPAP to give him a chance to breathe in room air again. The medication actually worked, and he passed the test, breathing on his own again. Praise God!

The next morning, the laryngoscopy specialist came in to see George. To my surprise, it was the same man who had brought me the bad report from Joy's condition. My heart dropped when I saw him. He came in and just stood there. He didn't touch George, as he looked at the monitors. Turning finally towards me, he said, "I think George wanted to meet me," and he walked away. I was shocked, and speechless. "That's all you have to say?"

Shortly after this, the doctor's rounds began, and a plan was set to take George off the CPAP and to try nasal prongs with a slow flow of humidified air.

I was overwhelmed with excitement. I called my husband and he started thanking God for this wonderful news. Hearing good news, every now and then, gave me joy. After the doctors met to discuss George's condition, the machine was taken away and the new plan was to send us back to the South Health Campus within the next two days.

This time, George was admitted to bed number 33. Everything was going well with the bottle feeding, but as a precaution, the feeding tube was kept in.

Three weeks passed, and weight gain was evident. It was then that George started exhibiting Anaemia.

Anaemia is a condition that is caused by a lack of red blood cells. It means that the body's tissues and organs cannot get enough oxygen. Red blood cells are given this colour by a red protein molecule called hemoglobin. This protein is responsible for transporting oxygen around the body. As the doctor was explaining this, all I could think of was why is there yet another issue?

George was getting worse day by day again, and the only option for him was to get a blood transfusion. I honestly thought that my happy life was over.

I said to the doctor, "There is no way. I am not allowing my baby to have another person's blood. Impossible!" I was so upset and irritated, that I was beyond holding myself together. I felt stuck at the hospital, losing my mind and had forgotten that my baby was not doing well. My husband, who is very wise (bless his heart), gently said, "Let's calm down and pray about this."

A blood transfusion is generally the process of receiving blood intravenously. Babies who are born premature, sometimes need more than one blood transfusion just to boost their red blood cell count, but most of the time, they are fine with just a one-time transfusion.

CHAPTER 20

FORMULA SWITCH

My erroneous fear was that whoever's blood was used for George, would stay in his system and mess up his DNA. Thank you to the nurses and doctors, who took their time educating me, and with the help of internet, I learned that blood doesn't last forever, and that these cells have a typical life span of 120 days. I was so happy to know that the donor's blood would remain only for a short span. I immediately communicated back to my husband and the doctors, and the papers for the transfusion process began. I only agreed for the sake of saving baby George. The next day, he was transfused, and within hours, he was back to himself, alert and attentive.

Everyone was so happy that he was doing great, and we went back to bottle feeding training again. To everyone's surprise, this caused specks of blood in his stools. "Not again! **Really, what else could go wrong with this kid?"**

Blood tests were taken, as well as an ultrasound and x-ray. The doctors came to the conclusion that it was the breast milk causing the problem. We then eliminated feeding him breast milk, because of the possibility of allergies. We then introduced Nutramigen formula, which he completely disliked.

I lost faith and the hope of ever going home. I truly felt like the hospital was my habitation now. My kids missed me so much, because I would leave to be with baby George from 8:00 AM to 10:00 or 11:00 PM. Sometimes, I would be away longer if I slept there. I thought that nothing could go wrong if I stayed by his side, but of course, that is not true. Anything can happen with or without you there.

Thank you to 'Meals Made by Momma,' as there was always food available for me to eat if I had forgotten to pack a lunch, or had to stay longer than expected.

George didn't have any more issues with blood in his stools after switching to the Nutramigen formula, but there soon appeared to be issues with his little tummy, which forced us to try another formula called Neocate. This formula is more broken down, containing very little dairy. The Neocate formula worked well and before we knew it, George was back on his bottle feeding training again, which took him only a week to adjust to.

This journey was just as painful for me, yet the ending was a happy result.

CHAPTER 21

MISSION ACOMPLISHED – DREAM FULFILLED

On November 21, 2016, at 2:50 PM, George was released to go home, after exactly 69 days of a painful journey. What I had longed for had finally come to pass. I couldn't believe the doctor when he said, "Take your baby home and make sure he stays at home for now." I was thrilled, and overwhelmed with joy and happiness. Tears were rolling down my face, and all I could say was. "Thank you Lord for giving a happy ending to my painful, frustrating, and emotional journey, which I will never forget."

With being at the NICU for 69 days, I sometimes thought that I would never go home. I actually believed that there were some doctors out to get me, and were making me stay at the hospital on purpose. Of course, that is not true. I have come to find out that the doctors take pleasure in sending families home. No doctor wants their patients, especially children, to remain at the hospital. If you feel the same way as I had felt, I know that your journey can be an easier one, knowing that someone has gone before you and weeded out all of the lies that will go through your mind.

Everything has its season, and going home with your baby is what you need to hang on to. For the mothers, who have been told that there is no chance of leaving the hospital, be encouraged, because the medical teams are the best in your hospital, and things can turn around for the good in a second.

I would like to encourage families that have lost a child, to not give up on your dreams of having more children. We go through things for a reason, even though at the time, it will not make much sense.

To parents who have had a baby with a life-threatening medical condition, please concentrate on the positive results, and do not focus on the bad reports. I did focus on the negative and it affected me greatly.

Every morning, I remember the doctors going from one room to another, which in the hospital world, is called 'rounds.' This ritual started between 9:30 AM and 10 AM, and baby George was always the last or the sixth baby to be seen by the doctors. I was usually anxious and restless, because plans and decisions were made after the doctors discussed the progress of the baby.

I would always remember the bad report because it was that report that was holding us back from going home. When I realized that focusing on the negative was discouraging me too much, I started to begin appreciating the good progress, and that helped me to remain strong and steadfast.

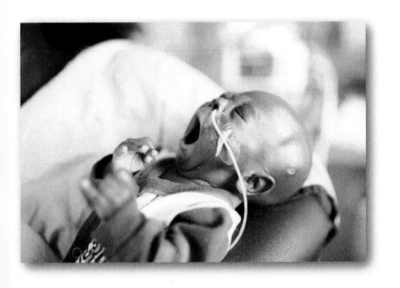

CHAPTER 22

NEVER ALONE

It is okay to cry and ask questions. It's okay to feel like your world is falling apart. It is all part of the process, but don't stay there for very long. Wipe your tears after crying, and stand up again. Don't lose hope and don't give up. Take time to search your heart and make the best decision for your child.

To the husbands and fathers, your support is greatly needed. To be honest, if it wasn't for my dear husband, I think I would have given up on everything, because I was carried away by my emotions. My husband pulled me right back to his arms, making sure that I was not going to lose my mind. He stood by my side, cooked, cleaned, and sometimes, put me to bed.

I would encourage the men to not take anything personal from their wives, because most women speak out of a grieving heart, over the situation that they are facing.

For those who are having a hard time understanding or getting along with the doctors, take your time to know them and their terms. **They are not your enemies. They are your teammates, so tag along beside them. Your**

frustrations will be easier, as you try to put yourself in their shoes. When I started putting my ego and frustrations aside, everything became easier for me. I tried to understand the medical terms, and if I couldn't understand them, I asked the nurses. Communication is the key to everything. Shutting yourself out, and not sharing how you feel about certain decisions that are being made by the medical team, will only make your journey that more difficult.

Doctors want you to ask your questions. They want to relinquish your fears and concerns. They want you to express your feelings. Your understanding and misunderstandings are meant to be communicated. It is only then that you will be helped in a healthy way.

For those of us who are not from Canada, and where English is not our first language, we can use the excuse that our culture and little English doesn't allow us to communicate properly.

This is very true, but we must not let that hinder our understanding. In cultures, like mine for example, it does not allow for me to have eye contact with others, and it does not allow debate with people, who are educated above us, such as doctors. We are in Canada, and everything we do is all about communication.

If you cannot speak English, there are translators or interpreters to be found. They will help with the language spoken by the doctors and nurses. For you and your family's mental health, it is vital for you to clearly understand what the doctor is relaying, in order to make the best decisions possible. English is not my first language either. I remember when I started school, and didn't even know how to say 'hi,' but I had a desire to know and to understand English.

To mothers who have just had a baby, and are still in the hospital, soon to go home, be strong and know that you are not alone. Take the time to look around and ask other mothers what their story is. You can do this in the same lunch room, or NICU hallway. By relating to that woman, you can share your heartbreaks, and come together to create the strength that is needed. I did this and I came to know many mothers who had to say goodbye to their newborn babies. There were other mothers too, who were clinging to the 60% chance of life with their baby who was only given a 40% chance to survive. I want to let you know that there is an expiration date to every crisis.

I would also like to encourage the mothers who have gone through trauma and have put their dreams of studying, or expanding their family on hold. I believe that it is possible for your dreams to come to pass. The pain of bad memories will haunt you, but continue pursuing your goals with a passion to reach the stars. I never thought that I would have any more kids after Joy's death, but here I am with four beautiful children, who fill my life with laughter, and happiness. I cannot imagine my life without them. I pray that the ending to your story will be as happy as mine.

In conclusion, when it comes to life and death, you and I have no control, and we cannot decide who will live or die. Life and death is beyond you and me. We can try to save a life, but if it's meant to die, we need to accept that outcome as well. It is among the most painful circumstances where we require hope.

We need to always believe for better results, because where there is hope, there is a new path. This path may look or feel bumpy, but it is a path that you will need to keep walking on. Eventually, it will clear, and you will see your dreams coming to pass right before your eyes.

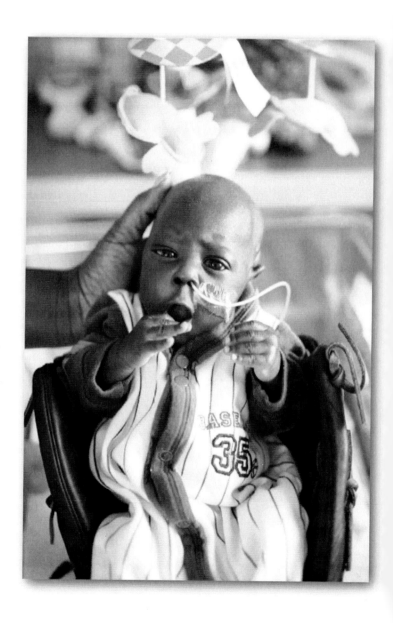

CHAPTER 23

PRAYER

I *pray for every baby in the incubator right now that is supported by any type of machine. I pray for each day to go as planned, and that there will be protection for each baby from any form of infection or illness. May these little bodies be strengthened through Your mighty power.*

Prayer for the Doctors and Nurses

I pray that You will give the doctors and nurses the skill to do all that is needed to care for these babies. May You reward them for their hard work of saving lives. I pray that You will bless and strengthen them each day.

Prayer for Mothers

Give the mothers the sufficient strength that can only come from You, and may Your peace fill their hearts knowing that all things work together for good to those that are called according to Your good purpose. When confusion and the spirit of death is so close, please hide them under the shadow of Your wings.

Prayer for Fathers

I thank you Lord for fathers, as they are the head of their families. They sometimes try their best to be strong in the moment where crisis has attacked their families. May You give them wisdom and empower them to make the right decision at the right time. May they never grow weary and weak. May they mount up with wings like eagles and may their strength be renewed each day.

IN JESUS MIGHTY NAME!
AMEN

IF you enjoyed this book, and believe that it would be helpful to any of the below, please feel free to share my story by obtaining a copy of this book for them, or contacting me at the information provided. 🖤

- **Daughter**
- **Someone thinking of abortion**
- **Friend**
- **Grieving mother**
- **Pregnant women in crisis**
- **NICU worker**
- **Pregnancy Centers**
- **Social Worker**
- **Counsellor**
- **Grieving father**
- **Parents of sick children**
- **Women Centers**
- **Hospitals near you**
- **Teenagers**
- **Pastor's wife**

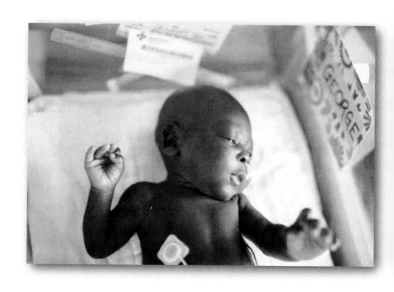

ABOUT THE AUTHOR

Akeir M.J. is a family and youth counselor, and also helps her husband, who is a Pastor at CrossPointe Miracles Centre Church in Canada, where she lives with him and their four children: two sons and two daughters. *69 Days in the NICU* is her first book.

QUESTIONS FOR THE DOCTOR

1) _____

_____

_____

_____

_____

_____

_____

_____

_____

_____

_____

_____

2) _____

_____

_____

_____

_____

_____

_____

_____

_____

_____

_____

_____

_____

_____

_____

3) _____

_____

_____

_____

_____

_____

_____

_____

_____

_____

_____

_____

4) _____

_____

_____

_____

_____

_____

_____

_____

_____

_____

_____

_____

_____

QUESTIONS FOR THE NURSE

1) _____

_____

_____

_____

_____

_____

_____

_____

_____

_____

_____

_____

2) _____

_____

_____

_____

_____

_____

_____

_____

_____

_____

_____

_____

_____

3)_____

_____

_____

_____

_____

_____

_____

_____

_____

_____

_____

_____

4)_____

_____

_____

_____

_____

_____

_____

_____

_____

_____

_____

_____

_____

Your personal prayer

_____

_____

_____

_____

_____

_____

_____

_____

_____

_____

_____

_____

_____

_____

_____

_____

_____

_____

_____

_____

_____

_____

Journal

Journal

Journal

Journal